CLOTTED CREAM FUDGE
HEINZ

Harvest Festival

Diana Bentley
Reading Consultant
University of Reading

Photographs by
Tim and Jennie Woodcock

Wayland

My School

Christmas
The Class Teacher
The Dinner Ladies
Harvest Festival
The Lollipop Man
The Road Safety Officer
The School Caretaker
The School Fête
The School Outing
The School Secretary

First published in 1988 by
Wayland (Publishers) Limited
61 Western Road, Hove
East Sussex, BN3 1JD, England

British Library Cataloguing in Publication Data
Bentley, Diana
Harvest festival.
1. Harvest festivals – For children
I. Title II. Woodcock, Tim
III. Woodcock, Jennie IV. Series
394.2′683

ISBN 1 85210 513 5

Phototypeset by
Kalligraphics Limited
Redhill, Surrey
Printed and bound by
Casterman S.A., Belgium

Contents

Today we are having a harvest festival	8
We all bring some food into school	10
We say thank you for the food	12
We collect up the food	14
We take the food to old people	16
Jonathan gives food to an old lady	18
Our class make bean and seed patterns	20
We make potato cut-outs	22
Some of us paint cards	24
Fazal draws a tomato	26
Glossary	28
Books to read	29
Index	30

All the words that appear in **bold** are explained in the glossary on page 28.

Hello, today we are
having a harvest festival.

Harvest time is **celebrated** all over the world. It is a time when we say thank you for all the food we are given. The farmers have grown the **crops** and we will eat them during the next year. Today we are looking at some of them.

We all bring some food into school.

Everyone brings some food to school. At the morning **assembly** we bring in bread, fruit, vegetables, jam and tins of food. At the front of the assembly hall is a long table. We put all the food on it. There are also some pretty flowers. Jeanette is bringing in a large loaf of bread.

Tetley
Knorr
HEINZ
FAMILY PACK

At assembly we say thank you for the food.

We have a school assembly. We say thank you for the food that is collected at harvest. Atia stands at the front of the hall and reads to us. Afterwards we sing a song together.

Granulated sugar
PG tips
80 Flavour Flow Tea Bags
OXO
KOUNTY KIST
WHOLE KERNEL CORN
SAINSBURY'S
Spaghetti

We collect up the food.

After assembly we collect up the food. We each have a plastic bag. We put some food in each bag. Nishan has got two tins in his hands. Most of the food has already gone. There isn't much left on the table.

We take food to the old people.

Sarah, Jonathan, Louise and Vassa are going to take some food to old people who live nearby. A policeman helps the children to find their **addresses**.

Jonathan gives food to an old lady.

Jonathan is going to give his food to the lady who lives in this house. He walks up the path and rings the bell. The others wait at the gate. Jonathan gives the lady everything in his bag. She is very pleased with it.

Our class make bean and seed patterns.

Back at school we have collected lots of different beans and seeds. Alison and Fiona have pieces of paper with glue on them. They make patterns on the paper with the beans and seeds. These two boys are also making patterns.

WHY
PRICES TO
MAKE YOU

We make potato cut-outs.

Have you ever made pictures with a potato? Soraya and Stephen are doing this. They have cut potatoes in half and cut out patterns on the bottom. Then they dip the potato in coloured paints. When they press the potato on the paper it leaves a potato print. Walid is using blue and yellow paints to make his pattern.

Some of us paint cards.

Some of us paint cards to celebrate harvest. Everyone paints a letter of the **alphabet**. Nishan has painted an 'H'. After it he has written 'Harvest is the time when we bring food to school'. When all the cards are painted we will put them on the wall.

Fazal draws a tomato.

There are many different kinds of fruit and vegetables. Do you know what all these ones are? Fazal is drawing a tomato. He has cut it in half and is drawing what it looks like inside. Harvest time is a good time to learn about some of the food that we eat.

Glossary

Address The name or number of a house, and the street and town it is in.

Alphabet All the letters used in a language, arranged in a special order.

Assembly A time when the school gathers together.

Celebrate When we remember a happy occasion.

Crops A general name for the things that grow on a farm, such as wheat, fruit and vegetables.

Harvest A time when the crops are picked and stored for the winter.

Books to read

Harvest and Thanksgiving by Ralph Whitlock (Wayland, 1984)
My class at Harvest Festival by Ruth Thomson (Franklin Watts, 1986)

Acknowledgement
The author and publishers would like to thank the head teacher, staff and pupils of Belmont Junior School, Wood Green, London.

Index

activities 20–27
assembly 10, 12, 13, 15, 28

bread 10

cards 24, 25
celebrations 9, 25, 28
crops 9, 28

farmers 9
fruit 10, 27

harvest 9, 25, 27, 28

jam 10

old people 16, 19

paints 23
patterns 20, 23
potato prints 22, 23

singing 13

tinned food 10, 15

vegetables 10, 27